MARTIN LUTHER

An Ecumenical Perspective

WALTER KASPER

Translated by **William Madges**

Paulist Press
New York / Mahwah, NJ

Cover image (background) by zeffss/Bigstock.com
Cover design by Dawn Massa, Lightly Salted Graphics
Book design by Lynn Else

Library of Congress Control Number: 2016950739

ISBN 978-0-8091-5320-6 (paperback)
ISBN 978-1-58768-692-4 (e-book)

Published by Paulist Press
997 Macarthur Boulevard
Mahwah, New Jersey 07430

www.paulistpress.com

Printed and bound in the
United States of America

MARTIN LUTHER

For my sister Ingeborg
Called home by God on January 28, 2016

CONTENTS

THE MANY PORTRAITS OF LUTHER AND LUTHER THE STRANGER

There are only a few historical personages like Martin Luther, the memory of whom appeals to both friend and foe alike, even after five hundred years. Our ideas about Martin Luther have changed in many ways over these five hundred years: Luther as Reformer; as the church father of Protestantism; as the standard-bearer of reason and freedom; as a brave German national hero; and many others. There are as many portraits of Luther as there are books about him.[1]

For Catholics, Luther was for a long time simply the heretic to blame for the division of the Western Church and all of the bad consequences of that division that continue to today. Those times are by and large past. Catholic research of Luther made a significant turn in the twentieth century, which resulted in recognition of Luther's genuine religious concerns, a fairer judgment of his responsibility for dividing the church, the reception of many of his insights under the banner of ecumenism, and—not least of all—the reception of his hymns.[2] Recent popes have adopted this point of view. Pope Benedict did so during his visit on September 23, 2011, to the chapter hall of the Augustinian cloister in Erfurt, where Luther took his monastic vows. Luther has almost become a common church father for many people.

The numerous opinions published by the Evangelical Church in Germany marking the 500th anniversary of the Reformation do not go that far. While they all take into account the change in the ecumenical perception of Luther, they also state that between the churches controversial questions still remain.[3] Therefore, many Christians rightly expect that the commemoration of five hundred years of Reformation in the year 2017 will bring us one step closer to the goal of ecumenical unity. We must not disappoint this expectation.

Luther himself was no proponent of ecumenism. Toward the end of his life, he no longer considered agreement with Rome possible. He could have scarcely imagined that Catholic Christians today sing his hymns in their church services. Nor could he envision our dialogue with the Jews, about whom he spoke in a derogatory way that is highly distressing for us; nor our dialogue with Muslims, to whom he did not show himself favorably disposed in his treatises against the Turks; and not our dialogue with the Anabaptists, and today with the Baptists and Mennonites, who back then were persecuted by Protestants as well as Catholics.

The strangeness goes even deeper. For many people today, including many practicing Christians of both churches, the questions that Luther raised are not at all still comprehensible. That is true for many Catholics with regard to indulgences; and it is true for many Protestants with regard to the justification of the sinner. In a world in which God often has become a stranger, both issues have become foreign to many of our contemporaries. The word *church* for many, still more than was already the case for Luther, is a completely *meaningless and obscure word.*[4]

Before we speak of Luther's relevance today, we must engage with his person and work to locate him in the changed situation of both churches and ecumenism. We have to be aware of the strangeness of the world in which Luther lived, as well as the strangeness of his message. I will argue that it is precisely the strangeness of Luther and his message that makes him so relevant to ecumenical relations today.

NOTES

1. Concerning the changes in the Protestant understanding of Luther, see Bernhard Lohse, *Martin Luther: An Introduction to His Life and Work* (Philadelphia: Fortress Press, 1986), 199–237. Of the more recent Protestant presentations, the following have been important to me: Volker Leppin, *Martin Luther* (Darmstadt: Wissenschaftliche Buchgesellschaft, 2010); Heinz Schilling, *Martin Luther: Rebell in einer Zeit des Umbruchs* (Munich: Beck, 2014); and a critical Protestant view by Hans-Martin Barth, *Die Theologie Martin Luthers: Eine kritische Würdigung* (Gütersloh: Gütersloher Verlagshaus, 2009).

2. The negative Catholic portrait of Luther that predominated for a long time was established by Johannes Cochlaeus. Heinrich Denifle demonized Luther and Hartmann Grisar pathologized him, but historical self-criticism (as represented by the work of Sebastian Merkle and Adolf Herte) led Joseph Lortz, Hubert Jedin and their students (especially Erwin Iserloh and Otto Hermann Pesch, among others) to acknowledge Luther's religious concern. An extensive presentation of the state of research can be found in the publication of the Ecumenical Working Group, *Reformation 1517–2017: Ökumenische Perspektiven* (Freiburg: Herder, 2014).

3. Above all: *Vom Konflikt zur Gemeinschaft: Gemeinsames lutherisch-katholisches Reformationsgedenken im Jahr 2017.* Bericht der Lutherisch/Römisch-katholischen Kommission für die Einheit (Leipzig: Evangelische Verlagsanstalt, 2013); Church Council of the Protestant Church in Germany, *Rechtfertigung und Freiheit: 500 Jahre Reformation 2017: Ein Grundlagentext des Rates der Evangelischen Kirche in Deutschland* (Gütersloh: Gütersloher Verlagshaus, 2014); Dorothea Sattler, *Reformation 1517–2017: Ökumenische Perspektiven. Für den Ökumenischen Arbeitskreis evangelischer und katholischer Theologen* (Freiburg im Breisgau: Herder, 2014).

4. Thus Martin Luther, "On the Councils and the Church" (1539), in *Luther's Works*, Vol. 41: *Church and Ministry III*, ed. Eric W. Gritsch (Philadelphia: Fortress Press, 1966), 144. *D. Martin Luthers Werke*, Kritische Gesamtausgabe (Weimar: Hermann Böhlau, 1883–2009), 50:625. Hereafter this critical edition of Luther's Works will be cited as WA.

Chapter 1

A TRANSITIONAL PERIOD OF DECLINE AND NEW BEGINNINGS

The world into which Martin Luther was born on November 10, 1483, is alien to us today. It was the conclusion, the "autumn of the Middle Ages" (Johan Huizinga), with undeniably many abuses in the church; above all, an externalization of piety. The demand for a reform of the church in head and members was everywhere present and the need for reform was also raised time and again by imperial diets. It was the autumnal time of decline. The reputation of the papacy had suffered terribly because of the Western Schism (1378–1417), when, for a while, three popes opposed one another as rivals and mutually excommunicated each other. Considerable ambiguity dominated theology, especially with regard to the doctrine of grace of William of Ockham's new movement (*via nova*)—nominalism. Luther came to know this doctrine primarily through Gabriel Biel, who became his archenemy in the doctrine of justification.[1]

On the other hand, many experienced the fifteenth century as the beginning of a new epoch: the discovery of the new world in America by Vasco da Gama and Columbus; the conquest of Constantinople (1453) that ended the millennial reign of the Byzantine Empire; the recapture of Granada (1492) and definitive expulsion of Islam from Spain that ended the Reconquest; Johannes Gutenberg's

(1400–1468) development of the art of printing; Copernicus's (1473–1543) discovery that Earth revolves around the sun—all of this contributed to many feeling they were at the beginning of a new age. All in all, it was therefore a time of transition, a "saddle period" (Reinhart Koselleck) in which the old and the new encountered each other, overlapped, and came into conflict.

Luther can be understood only within the context of this tension between the Middle Ages and the modern era. He was a person of his time, not ours. This transitional quality is also evident in the church of his time. There was decline and decay, but there also existed a Catholic Reform before the Reformation: in Spain, a national council in Seville (1478) did away with the sale of indulgences, an abuse that later led to the Reformation; the famous Polyglot, the multilingual Bible of Alcalá, was published there; various reform groups and reform religious orders arose in Italy. One speaks of an Italian *evangelism*, a movement of renewal on the basis of the gospel that reached into the highest ecclesial circles of the curia (Cardinal Gasparo Contarini, Reginald Pole).

Besides much discontent concerning the pope and the curia, which financially drained the country, we find in Germany a new lay piety (*devotio moderna*) that Martin Luther became familiar with as a student in Marburg. Luther also shared his culture's lively interest in mysticism, especially that of Johannes Tauler (died 1361). Interest in the Bible had been aroused even before Luther. There is evidence of German translations of the Bible before the Reformation. Luther did not join a run-down religious order, but rather joined the reform order of Augustinian monks in Erfurt. His spiritual mentor, Johannes von Staupitz, taught him the renewal movement associated with Augustine and Bernard of Clairvaux, a mystical piety that distinguished itself from an externalized piety.[2] One can characterize the young Luther, so to speak, as a Reform Catholic.

The emergence of Renaissance humanism had the widest reach. When Constantinople fell, many Byzantine scholars fled to Italy. A new interest in the ancient world was awakened. The cry *ad fontes*, "back to the sources," meant that Holy Scripture was no longer read through the lens of scholasticism, but rather in the original Hebrew and Greek languages. Luther was also significantly influenced by this. It was equally essential for Renaissance humanism that the human being and his dignity took center stage (Pico della Mirandola). In this way, the modern period, the modern self-understanding of the human person, and the modern attitude toward life was established.

The spokesperson of Christian humanism was Erasmus of Rotterdam (died 1536), who was highly educated and regarded in all of Europe. He did not spare sanctimonious Christians, hypocritical monks, and corrupt popes his criticism. Wilhelm Dilthey called him the Voltaire of the sixteenth century.[3] In his *Philosophy of Christ*, he juxtaposed externalized piety to a renewal and reflection upon the essence of being Christian. He ran into sharp disagreement with Luther about this, which then took on fateful significance for the modern period. In the modern period in Europe, humanism and Reformation were two stars, mutually attracted in their spheres yet nevertheless diverging from each other.[4]

NOTES

1. I limit myself to the reference to the summary presentation in Erwin Iserloh, *Geschichte und Theologie der Reformation im Grundriss* (Paderborn: Bonifatius, 1980) and his *Kirche—Ereignis und Institution: Aufsätze und Vorträge*, vol. 2: *Geschichte und Theologie der Reformation* (Münster: Aschendorff, 1985).

2. The mystical side of Luther, especially the influence of Bernard of Clairvaux, is mostly underappreciated. The negative judgment of liberal theology, especially Adolf von Harnack's, continues to have an effect. Luther distinguishes himself from the liberal position through the ecstatic character of faith and the Word that encounters the human person "from the outside." In this way, he has developed a new type of mysticism, a mysticism of the Word and faith, which is not

reserved only for pious individuals. Luther, so to speak, democratized mysticism. See the works of E. Iserloh, H. Oberman, U. Köpf, V. Leppin, B. Hamm, and others, to which reference is made in Franco Buzzi, Dieter Kampen, and Paolo Ricca, eds., *Lutero e la mistica* (Turin: Claudiana, 2014). Concerning the influence of Bernard, see also Franz Posset, *The Real Luther: A Friar at Erfurt and Wittenberg. Exploring Luther's Life with Melanchthon as Guide* (Saint Louis: Concordia, 2011).

3. Wilhlem Dilthey, "Auffassung und Analyse des Menschen im 15. und 16. Jahrhundert," in *Gesammelte Schriften*, vol. 2, 2nd ed. (Leipzig and Berlin: Teubner, 1921), 42. See Peter Walter, *Theologie aus dem Geist der Rhetorik: Zur Schriftauslegung des Erasmus von Rotterdam* (Mainz: Matthias Grünewald, 1991).

4. Ernst Troeltsch, "Renaissance und Reformation," in *Gesammelte Schriften*, vol. 4 (Tübingen: J. C. B. Mohr, 1925), 261–96.

Chapter 2

LUTHER'S CONCERN: THE EVANGELICAL RENEWAL OF CHRISTIANITY

The prior short overview of the situation raises the question: What was, in fact, new about Luther and his reform? We would miss the point if we understood Luther's Ninety-Five Theses only as the last drop that caused the barrel of discontent with Rome to overflow. To be sure, Luther had a lively feeling for what moved the people of his age, but he was also a person greatly out of season. His agenda cannot simply be derived from the situation at that time. Luther conceived of everything from its religious depths. With the distinct power of his language, which could be blunt and crude to the point of hateful tirades, but could just as well be pious, gentle, and profound, he addressed people's existential questions and reached their religious depth dimension. With incredible force, he placed the question about God, the most fundamental of all questions, at the center.[1]

"How do I get a gracious God?" That was Luther's existential problem, which troubled him personally. On the occasion of Johann Tetzel's preaching concerning indulgences, it became for him a pastoral problem in the confessional because he saw that the preaching about indulgences communicated a deceitful certainty about salvation, as if one could be redeemed in God's eyes by means of indulgences. Ultimately for him, as a doctor of Holy

Scripture, the question about a gracious God became a matter of interpreting the *iustitia Dei* in Romans 1:17: "In the gospel the righteousness of God is revealed from faith for faith; as it is written, 'The one who is righteous will live by faith.'" (*Lectures on Romans* 1515/1516)[2]

Luther discovered that the righteousness of God is not an active, retributive, punitive, and vengeful righteousness, but rather is a passive, forgiving, and consoling righteousness that makes a person just and thereby makes him or her free. This righteousness becomes ours not on account of our human works but exclusively on account of God's grace and mercy; not through external forms of piety, such as indulgences, but rather through faith. In this way, against the then current externalization of Christian existence, Luther focused on the internalization of Christian existence, a deeply mystical concern.

In retrospect of his later years, Luther characterized this knowledge, what became known as his "tower experience," as his Reformation breakthrough.[3] With this breakthrough we are probably dealing not with a dateable experience, but rather with a longer process of clarification and awareness. Contemporary Catholic research on Luther since Joseph Lortz has come to the judgment that, in his debate with Ockham's viewpoint and in reliance on Augustine, Luther vanquished a Catholicism that was not really Catholic and consequently rediscovered something that was primordially Catholic.[4]

Therefore, behind Luther's Ninety-Five Theses of 1517—regardless of whether he really nailed them to the door of the Wittenberg Castle Church or sent them out—stands a thoroughly Catholic concern. The theses about indulgences were conceived not as a revolutionary document, but rather as an invitation to an academic discussion, which never took place. For the most part, they remained within the parameters of what was then tenable in theology, and are a document of reform but not of the Reformation.[5] This reform pertained to the renewal of the Catholic Church and the renewal of all of Christianity; it did not have its own Reform church as a goal. The theses became the source of a Reformation movement only by means of the echo, which surprised and over-powered even Luther himself. They unleashed a historical dynamic, which changed Luther from actor to spectator and made him to be the one being driven and pushed.

Luther's concern was the gospel of the glory of God's grace, *quod est maximum* [which is the greatest]. For Luther, the gospel was not a book, not even the Bible or a code of doctrines, but rather a living message, which becomes a personal existential address, a word of assurance, and a promise (*promissio*) for me (*pro me*) and for us (*pro nobis*).[6] It is the message of the cross, which alone grants peace. In his rejection of works of righteousness, Luther was concerned with anything but a cheap Christendom at discount prices. Right in the first thesis, he says that the entire life of a Christian must be a constant act of contrition. Consequently, from the very beginning, Luther's reform stood in the context of his theology of repentance and "our Lord and Master Jesus'" call to conversion.

In this way, Luther was a reform-minded person [*Reformer*], not a Reformer [*Reformator*]. He was not thinking of becoming the founder of a separate Reform church. His goal was the renewal of the Catholic Church from the perspective of the gospel. As his early letters show, he was concerned about the knowledge of Christ (*cognitio Christi*) and only about Christ (*solus Christus*). He said that we wanted to let the light of the gospel shine forth again in his heart out of the darkness in which it had been held hidden. With all of his occasionally pointed statements, that was a wake-up call and an offer of the Holy Spirit to the church.

With this evangelical concern—in the original sense of the word—Luther stood in the long line of Catholic figures of renewal who preceded him. One can think above all of Francis of Assisi, who wanted simply to live the gospel with his brothers and thereby to preach it. One would speak today of the new evangelization.

We must reflect together in an ecumenical fashion on this original, evangelical, and Catholic concern of Luther.

NOTES

1. Concerning Luther's doctrine of God and the trinity, see Bernhard Lohse, *Martin Luther: An Introduction to His Life and Work* (Philadelphia: Fortress Press, 1986), 165–74.

2. Wilhelm Pauck, ed. and trans., *Luther: Lecture on Romans* (Philadelphia: Westminster, 1961), 17–19.

3. Concerning the much-discussed Reformation breakthrough, see Lohse, *Martin Luther: An Introduction to His Life and Work*, 149–53. In the debate about this question, there is the danger of making a circular argument, in which one presupposes one element is a Reformation element and another is Catholic, from which the Reformation element has removed itself.

4. This is the position of Iserloh, *Kirche—Ereignis und Institution*, 145–55.

5. The Johann-Adam Möhler Institut in Paderborn, together with the Strasbourg Institute for Ecumenical Research, is planning an ecumenical commentary on Martin Luther's Ninety-Five Theses.

6. Martin Luther, "On the Bondage of the Will," in *Luther and Erasmus: Free Will and Salvation*, eds. E. Gordon Rupp and Philip S. Watson (Philadelphia: Westminster, 1969), 210, 213–14; WA 18:682, 692, 695; cf. *Augsburg Confession*, Article V, in *The Book of Concord: The Confessions of the Evangelical Lutheran Church*, trans. and ed. Theodore G. Tappert (Philadelphia: Fortress Press, 1959), 31. This understanding comes close to that of Thomas Aquinas, who himself came from the evangelical reform movement of Francis of Assisi and Dominic. See his *Summa theologiae*, I-II, q. 106, a. 1 and 2.

Chapter 3

THE BEGINNING OF THE AGE OF DENOMINATIONS AND ITS END

B efore we consider the contemporary relevance of Luther's original concern, we must ask how the division of Christianity came about, with all of its bad consequences, rather than its renewal. Wolfhart Pannenberg has rightly said: the emergence of an independent Lutheran church is not a sign of success; rather, it signifies the failure of the Reformation.[1]

As is always the case with such questions, one can name a myriad of reasons. The Reformation is a highly complex, historical event for which one-sided recriminations do not advance our discussion. One reason is certain: Luther's call for repentance was not heard in Rome and by the bishops at that time. Instead of being penitent and responding with the necessary reforms, Luther was answered with polemic and condemnation. Rome bears its fill of complicity in the fact that a church-dividing Reformation developed out of the reform of the church. Pope Adrian VI already acknowledged this complicity through his legate at the Diet of Nuremberg in 1523.

After his interrogation by Cardinal Cajetan in Augsburg in 1518, then after the Leipzig Disputation with Johannes Eck in 1519, and finally after Rome's excommunication in 1521, the idea that the pope—who then was still Leo X who was opposed to *his* gospel—is the Antichrist foretold in 2 Thessalonians (2:4) was forced upon Luther because Rome and the bishops did not listen to the call for repentance and reform.[2] Luther was filled with an apocalyptic consciousness and saw himself engaged in the eschatological final battle between Christ and Antichrist.[3] That is a dangerous position. It rules out dialogue and permits no mediating positions. One cannot have a dialogue with the Antichrist, but only staunchly resist him. Thus, the monk and reform-minded Catholic, who in 1517, as a son of the church, pushed for reform and appealed to the pope, became the Reformer, even if he did not characterize himself that way. He became the one who, in order to introduce the course of reform, took over the helm itself only to turn it over to others soon after.

In his Reformation programmatic treatise of 1520, *To the Christian Nobility of the German Nation*,[4] Luther disputed the exclusive authority for reform claimed by the pope and the bishops, who were unwilling to do it. With reference to the statement of 1 Peter concerning the priesthood of all the baptized (2:5, 9), he developed the idea of the priesthood of all believers, which went far beyond the interpretation of the church fathers and high scholasticism to put into question the office of the pope and the Catholic understanding of church and office. In his second major treatise, again from the year 1520, *The Babylonian Captivity of the Church*[5], Luther than rejected the sacramental system of the Catholic Church as it was then represented to him.

Luther did not systematically sketch out a new understanding of the church. He was determined to introduce, in opposition to the deformations of the existing Roman system, a reform that corresponded to the original order. In reality, he introduced thereby a break with the Catholic understanding of church. He expressed the decisive point in his treatise to the nobility in the famous and often cited sentence: "For whoever comes out of the water of baptism can boast that he is already a consecrated priest, bishop, and pope, even though it is not fitting for just anyone to exercise such an office" (*To the Christian Nobility of the German Nation*).[6] For him the church was the assembly of the faithful, not the "corporeal" assembly, but the assembly of the "saints in faith" (*On the Papacy in Rome*, 1520).[7] As he said: "The church is hidden, the saints are unknown." (*On the Bondage of the Will*, *1526*).[8] In the process, the hierarchical conception was not simply denied, but became a question of second order, which can be skipped over for the sake of the gospel and, when appropriate, must be skipped over.

The break was symbolically completed with the burning of the bull that threatened his excommunication and the Code of Canon law at the Elster Gate of Wittenberg (1520). It was legally completed with his excommunication in 1521. His stance before the Diet in Worms (1521)—later shortened and circulated in this form by himself—was: "Here I Stand, I cannot do otherwise, God help me. Amen." This was the confirmation of this break before the Emperor and the Empire.[9]

Nonetheless, many doors still remained open in 1521. In the writings of the early 1520s, Luther conveyed the impression, from his polemical position, that ecclesial office is a necessary delegation of the common priesthood for the sake of order. He overcame this impression in his later writings. The mature Luther understood ecclesial office as a sign of the true church; he emphasized the institution of the office through Jesus Christ and he emphasized the significance of ordination.[10]

This position is incorporated in the *Augsburg Confession* (1530), in which Melanchthon attempted to come to agreement with the pope and the emperor. He gave indications that he was ready to recognize the historical office of bishop as the norm insofar as it made room for the gospel.[11] When this attempt failed, Luther surrendered the hope for possible unity. "Thus we are and remain eternally separated and against one another" (*Schmalkaldic Articles*, 1537),[12] he wrote at that time, because the pope in 1536 summoned a general council, first in Mantua, then in Trent, but far too late as developments had already advanced too far.

Not only theological, but also political reasons were decisive for this development. Already in 1520, Luther, on the basis of his teaching of the common priesthood, placed the reform in the hands of the Christian nobility and the magistrates of the imperial cities. The appeal to the nobility rather than to the people shows how very much Luther still thought in a medieval fashion. At the Diet of Speyer in 1526, the princes took the reform in hand. For Luther, the princes' reform was a stopgap measure and an emergency arrangement that had become necessary on account of the failure of the bishops.[13] Luther was convinced of the self-implementation of the word of God, *ubi et quando visum est Deo* [where and when it pleases God] (*Augsburg Confession*).[14] There was, as a result, a fundamental openness to the future. However, the emergency measure became a permanent arrangement for centuries, which led to the sovereign governance of the churches by the princes.

In the Peace of Augsburg in 1555, the principle (which was later concisely expressed in the formula), *cuius regio, eius religio* [Whose region, his religion], became the law of the empire. The sovereigns, but not individual Christians, were free to decide in favor of the Catholic or the Lutheran religion. Now the church system came into being, in which there was little place for the religious freedom of the individual—a church discipline that was scarcely inferior to the Catholic discipline. The emergency measure thus became the normal arrangement for centuries, with the governance of churches by the sovereigns a permanent institution.

Thus, the Reformation led initially not into the modern period, but to a prolongation of the Middle Ages. One fundamental difference from the Middle Ages, though, was that now both of the medieval brackets of the empire, pope and emperor, dropped out. The end of the imperial-ecclesial universalism brought about an ecclesial and political particularism and pluralism, and nurtured a denominationally colored nationalism with many unhealthy consequences for Europe. Already during Luther's lifetime, and then completely after his death, ecclesial unity was dissolved even within the Reformation movement, the result being an unhealthy pluralism within Western Christianity and then within all of Christianity.

In the more recent research, one speaks of the formation of denominations, which is the process that after Luther's death led from a reform movement affecting the entire church to the Reformation and to separated denominational churches.[15] This process came to its theological conclusion in 1580 with the last Lutheran Confession, the *Book of Concord*. Paradoxically, the Augsburg Confession, which was supposed to promote unity, now became the *Magna Carta* of a separate church of a new type, a church based on a confession—a confessional church. In the consciousness and in the concrete praxis of the people, the distinction was slowly established. Only from the seventeenth century on did it acquire a militant character, often leading to hatred and prejudice.

Even the Catholic Church assumed denominational characteristics with the postconciliar *Tridentine Profession of Faith* (1564), however, without understanding itself as a confessional church. Primarily thanks to its spreading in the new world of Latin America and through missionary activity in Africa and Asia, especially by Francis Xavier, the Catholic Church escaped the danger of becoming a local, particular church.

The state-church situation of the Lutheran territorial churches was retained in principle in Germany until the end of the monarchy in 1918. After 1933, as Peter Brunner formulated it, it fell into an even worse state of dependence with the "German Christians."[16] In the Scandinavian countries and similarly in the *Church of England*, the state-church system continued in weakened form into the present.

The denominational age came to an end in 1918 with the end of the monarchy and the subsequent upheavals of the twentieth and twenty-first centuries. In our pluralistic situation, in which the confessional milieus are dissolved and the members of the different denominations self-evidently live next to one another, work together, and often live (and pray) with one another in the same family, and in light of the contemporary processes of individualization, denominational boundaries are permeable and the confessional controversies have become irrelevant for many Protestant and Catholic Christians. That may be regrettable, but it does not change the fact that the confessional age is irretrievably past and every attempt to revive it upon the ruins of the past is condemned to failure. Neither Catholic attempts at restoration nor the celebrations in the year 2017 will change anything about that in the longer term.

NOTES

1. Wolfhart Pannenberg, "Reformation und Einheit der Kirche," in *Beiträge zur Systematischen Theologie*, vol. 3: *Kirche und Ökumene* (Göttingen: Vandenhoeck & Ruprecht, 2000): 173–85; here 174f.

2. The Antichrist polemic was widespread in the Middle Ages, but with Luther it had a precise theological meaning. The accusation, therefore, is also included in Lutheran confessional statements: see Philip Melanchthon, "Apology of the Augsburg Confession," 217–18, and 268; "Smalcald Articles," 297, 300–1; "Treatise on the Power and Primacy of the Pope," 327–30; "The Formula of Concord," 614–15, all in *The Book of Concord: The Confessions of the Evangelical Lutheran Church*, trans. and ed. Theodore G. Tappert (Philadelphia: Fortress Press, 1959). See H. Meyer, "Das Papsttum bei Luther und in den lutherischen Bekenntnisschriften," in *Lehrverurteilungen— kirchentrennend?* vol. 3: *Materialien zur Lehre von den Sakramenten und vom kirchlichen Amt*, ed. Wolfhart Pannenberg (Freiburg im Breisgau: Herder, 1990), 306–28.

3. The title of Heiko Oberman's book is noteworthy: *Luther: Man Between God and the Devil* (New Haven, CT: Yale, 2006).

4. Martin Luther, "To the Christian Nobility of the German Nation," in *Martin Luther: Three Treatises*, trans. Charles M. Jacobs (Philadelphia: Fortress Press, 1960), 7–112; WA 6:381–469.

5. Martin Luther, "The Babylonian Captivity of the Church," trans. A. T. W. Steinhäuser, in *Martin Luther: Three Treatises*, 123–260; WA 6:497–573.

6. Luther, "To the Christian Nobility of the German Nation," 14; WA 6:408. Concerning the Catholic understanding of the common priesthood, see Walter Kasper, *The Catholic Church: Nature, Reality, and Mission* (New York: Bloomsbury, 2015), 197–219, 240–42.

7. Martin Luther, "On the Papacy in Rome, Against the Most Celebrated Romanist in Leipzig," in *Luther's Works*, vol. 39: *Church and Ministry I*, ed. Eric W. Gritsch (Philadelphia: Fortress Press, 1970), 65; WA 6:301.

8. *"abscondita est Ecclesia, latent sancti."* Martin Luther, "On the Bondage of the Will," in *Luther and Erasmus: Free Will and Salvation*, trans. and ed. Philip S. Watson (Philadelphia: Westminster Press, 1969), 158; WA 18:652.

9. Volker Leppin, *Martin Luther* (Darmstadt: Wissenschaftliche Buchgesellschaft, 2010), 177; Heinz Schilling, *Martin Luther: Rebell in einer Zeit des Umbruchs* (Munich: Beck, 2012), 223.

10. See Wolfhart Pannenberg, "Das kirchliche Amt in der Sicht der lutherischen Lehre," in *Lehrverurteilungen—kirchentrennend?* Band 3: *Materialien zur Lehre von den Sakramenten und vom kirchlichen Amt*, 286–305. Also see his *Systematic Theology*, vol. 3, trans. Geoffrey W. Bromiley (Grand Rapids: Eerdmans, 1998), 393–404. There one can also find a different interpretation of the Augsburg Confession, art. V.

11. *The Augsburg Confession*, Art. XXVIII. On the occasion of the four hundred fiftieth anniversary of the Augsburg Confession in 1980, the attempt was made once again to come to an agreement between the churches on this basis; this time too without tangible results. From the abundance of publications, see: Harding Meyer, Heinz Schütte, Hans-Joachim Mund, eds., *Katholische Anerkennung des Augsburgischen Bekenntnisses? Ein Vorstoß zur Einheit zwischen katholischer und lutherischer Kirche* (Frankfurt am Main, Lembeck, 1977); Bernhard Lohse and Otto Hermann Pesch, eds., *Das Augsburger Bekenntnis von 1530 damals und heute* (Munich: Kaiser, 1980); Joseph A. Burgess, *The Role of the Augsburg Confession: Catholic and Lutheran Views* (Philadelphia: Fortress, 1980).

12. The Smalcald Articles, in *The Book of Concord: The Confessions of the Evangelical Lutheran Church*, 294.

13. Melanchthon, "Apology of the Augsburg Confession," art. XIV, in *The Book of Concord: The Confessions of the Evangelical Lutheran Church*, 214–15.

14. *The Augsburg Confession*, art. V.

15. Ernst Walter Zeeden summarizes in *Konfessionsbildung: Studien zur Reformation, Gegenreformation und katholischen Reform* (Stuttgart: Klett-Cotta, 1985). See Heinz Schilling, ed., *Die reformierte Konfessionalisierung in Deutschland: Das Problem der "Zweiten Reformation"* (Gütersloh: Gütersloher Verlagshaus, 1986); Hans Klueting, *Das Konfessionelle Zeitalter: Europa zwischen Mittelalter und Moderne* (Darmstadt: Wissenschaftliche Buchgesellschaft, 2007).

16. Peter Brunner, *Vom Amt des Bischofs* (Berlin: Lutherisches Verlagshaus, 1955), 46.

Chapter 4

LUTHER AND THE SPIRIT OF THE MODERN ERA

Because Luther cannot be brought up to date in a denominational way, the question arises: How then? The attempts at a nondenominational updating were already made early on. All of the Reformation jubilees have claimed Luther as the forerunner and trailblazer of their respective age. Especially in Germany, the attempt is made today to interpret Luther and the Reformation in the context of the modern history of freedom. The motto "Here I stand, I cannot do otherwise, so help me God" serves as the expression of Luther's freedom and courage, an expression of walking upright with head held high over against ecclesial and political authority.

There is much that is right about this view. Nevertheless, talk about Luther as the trailblazer of the freedom of spirit and the standard-bearer of the modern age raises many questions.[1] In Worms, Luther's appeal to conscience was without a doubt an important step in the modern history of freedom, even if for him it was not a matter of appealing to an autonomous conscience but to one captive to the word of God. In the Peasants' War as in the dispute with the Anabaptists and the Radical Reformers, he did not defend subjective conscience, but deemed the intervention of the temporal authorities necessary. Luther still held firmly to the medieval idea of the religious unity of the *societas christiana*

[Christian society]. Our contemporary pluralistic society was not imaginable for him or for people generally at that time.[2]

Luther's debate with the humanist Erasmus goes right to the real theological heart of the problem. In his treatise *De servo arbitrio* [*On the Bondage of the Will*] (1525) he responds to Erasmus's *De libero arbitrio* [*On the Freedom of the Will*] (1524). With all desirable clarity, Luther drives home the point that the freedom that he proclaimed—the freedom of the Christian who had been freed by the grace of God—is not the optimistic, self-determined freedom that Renaissance humanism had established and that increasingly prevailed in modernity. On this point, Luther was concerned about the linchpin (*cardo*) of theology.[3] Therefore, he conducted the debate with a sharpness that could hardly be surpassed and with exaggerated formulas that, in part, were hard to take. He commented, for example, that human persons are, like a mount, ridden either by God or by the devil.[4] It is no surprise that it unleashed a true shockwave in the humanistic world of scholars at that time.[5]

De servo arbitrio was the Reformation clarion call against the optimistic illusion that the human person could attain salvation automatically on the basis of his/her freedom. In this way, to be sure in a polemically exaggerated way, the all-decisive theological question was posed concerning the relation of theonomy and autonomy and, at the same time, a clear boundary was drawn over against humanism. Only much later did one try to patch up the break. Luther's concentration of the appropriation of salvation in the personal certitude of faith has been interpreted as the foundation of a religion of interiority, by means of which Luther freed the gospel from its Babylonian captivity to the ecclesial, sacramental mediation of salvation.[6] Thus, one could, as it were posthumously, reconcile Luther with Erasmus and make him, in conjunction with Hegel, Leopold von Ranke, and Max Weber, the symbolic figure of free modern culture in a culturally Protestant way.

For a person who has grown up in southern Germany and

lives in the Roman world, the Protestant-Prussian writing of the history of the nineteenth century is difficult to understand. Even more recent research would only confirm this reservation.[7] The history of freedom did not begin in 1517. Biblical criticism, courageous critique of the church, and ecclesial efforts at reform existed in great numbers already in the fifteenth century. The entire history of the Middle Ages is a history of reforms. Even the Catholic Reform was not at all only the belated reaction to Luther's criticism. It was in the air for a long time. It has many roots of its own and it led to a worldwide, independent modern form of the Catholic Church.

After the Thirty Years' War (1618–1648), there arose a Baroque culture, above all in the Catholic territories in Germany, in Austria, Italy, and Spain, extending all the way to Latin America, which expressed modern subjectivity in music, the performing arts, and in the educational institutions of the Jesuits in a distinctly independent way.[8] And last but not least, that is true of modern Catholic spirituality and mysticism. Think of the Spiritual Exercises of Ignatius of Loyola, which are geared toward an existential decision, or think of Teresa of Avila's and John of the Cross' subjective mysticism of experience, or the worldly piety of Francis de Sales in his treatise *Philothea* (1608/9), one of the ten most purchased writings of world literature. Even Baroque scholasticism, with its question about the final ground of faith (*Analysis-fidei* doctrine), exhibits many typical traits of the modern period.

First and foremost, if one asks about the origin of the modern age, one cannot skip over a country like France, which became determinative of modernity. Descartes, often described as the father of modern thought, was, as a student in a Jesuit college, saturated at any rate with Catholic ideas; not to mention Blaise Pascal, and also the great French, Spanish, and Italian classical authors. Thus Ernst Troeltsch concludes "that precisely in the age of denominations the mother countries of modern civilization— Italy, France, also Spain—are Catholic."[9]

MARTIN LUTHER

Denominational Lutheranism was paternalistic. It was the Anabaptists, who were persecuted by ecclesial and temporal authorities, and the Free churches, influenced by Calvin, which opposed the fusion of church and temporal authority. They were the ones who proclaimed a regime of freedom on the basis of God-given human rights in the American Declaration of Independence (1776), already ten years before the French Revolution's Declaration of Human and Civil Rights (1789). Two hundred years earlier, the Dominican theologians of Salamanca had laid its foundations,[10] and Bartholomew de las Casas demanded it with his intervention on behalf of the rights of the Indians. Modernity, therefore, is not to be explained from a single origin or principle. It has many fathers and also many mothers.

All of that does not call into question Luther's significance. The Reformation was unquestionably an important link in the chain of connections of the sixteenth and subsequent centuries. Nevertheless, the Reformation cannot be focused on Luther in a one-sided way. When it is a question of the history of effects of Lutheranism, mention, at the very least, must be made of the humanistic-minded Melanchthon. Furthermore, there are numerous and very different paths, which all in their own ways lead to modernity. Such paths exist in both churches; in the Free churches; in the English and French Enlightenment, which freed themselves from ecclesial influence; as well as in the recently emerging natural sciences (Copernicus, Galileo).

When one looks at the relativizing and skeptical outcome of modernity in postmodernity in its totality, one can ask, in the end, whether it was really Luther, who vehemently championed assertoric statements against Erasmus, or if it was rather Erasmus, whom Luther accused of halfhearted relativism, who won the day. Luther pointed out to Erasmus that *Spiritus sanctus non est scepticus* [The Holy Spirit is no skeptic.] (*De servo arbitrio*).[11] Today Luther would presumably make many theologians take that statement to heart. Over against many a postmodern manifestation of the history of freedom, he would set the theonomous freedom of the Christian, who has been graciously freed and is captive to the word of God. With this "Christian distinction" (Romano Guardini), Luther is a stranger in the modern period and his ecumenical relevance resides precisely in this, his Christological focus.

NOTES

1. For a nuanced presentation of the complex problem of "Luther and Modernity," see Gerhard Ebeling, "Der kontroverse Grund der Freiheit: Zum Gegensatz von Luther-Enthusiasmus und Luther-Fremdheit in der Neuzeit," in *Lutherstudien*, vol. 3 (Tübingen: Mohr, 1985), 366–94.

2. Karl Lehmann, *Toleranz und Religionsfreiheit: Geschichte und Gegenwart in Europa* (Freiburg im Breisgau: Herder, 2015), 30–34.

3. Martin Luther, "On the Bondage of the Will," in *Luther and Erasmus: Free Will and Salvation*, trans. and ed. Philip S. Watson (Philadelphia: Westminster, 1969), 116; WA 18:614. Early letters show that Luther was critically engaged with Erasmus early on; the numerous statements in Table Talk leave no doubt about the enduring fundamental opposition between Luther and Erasmus. See WA BR 1, 70; 133f. among others.

4. Martin Luther, "On the Bondage of the Will," 140; WA 18:635.

5. Leppin, *Martin Luther*, 246–57.

6. Thus in Hegel, whose view was taken over by Harnack among others. See Hegel's *Lectures on the History of Philosophy*, trans. E.S. Haldane and Frances H. Simson, 3 vols. (New York: Humanities Press, 1963), 3:146–55. Adolf von Harnack, *What is Christianity?* trans. Thomas Bailey Saunders (Philadelphia: Fortress Press, 1986), 270.

7. Wilhlem Dilthey, "Auffassung und Analyse des Menschen im 15. und 16. Jahrhundert," in *Gesammelte Schriften*, vol. 2, 2nd ed. (Leipzig and Berlin: Teubner, 1921). Ernst Troeltsch, "Renaissance und Reformation," in *Gesammelte Schriften*, vol. 4 (Tübingen: J. C. B. Mohr, 1925): 261–96. Harm Klueting summarizes the results of the more recent research in *Luther und die Neuzeit* (Darmstadt: Primus, 2011).

8. For initial information, see G. Schwaiger and P. Walter,

"Barock I-III" in *Lexikon für Theologie und Kirche*, 2nd ed. (1994): 2:20–25.

9. Ernst Troeltsch, *Die Soziallehren der christlichen Kirchen und Gruppen* (1912), in *Gesammelte Schriften*, vol. 1 (Tübingen: J.C.B. Mohr, 1919), 601. Also see his "Renaissance und Reformation," in *Gesammelte Schriften*, vol. 4 (Tübingen: J. C. B. Mohr, 1925): 289.

10. Joseph Höffner, *Christentum und Menschenwürde: Das Anliegen der spanischen Kolonialethik im Goldenen Zeitalter* (Trier: Paulinus, 1947); Brian Tierney, *The Idea of Natural Rights: Studies on Natural Rights, Natural Law, and Church Law 1150–1625* (Grand Rapids: Eerdmans, 1997).

11. Martin Luther, "On the Bondage of the Will," 109; WA 18:605.

Chapter 5

THE ECUMENICAL AGE AS THE REDISCOVERY OF CATHOLICITY

C arl Andresen, one of the most prominent Protestant experts in church history, has pointed to another frame of reference for an updated classification of Luther, which until now has received much too little attention.[1] In his *Handbook of the History of Dogmas and Theology*, he divides doctrinal development into three periods: the period of Catholicity (patristics and the Middle Ages), the period of confessionalism, and the period of ecumenicity [*Ökumenizität*].

The period of ecumenicity does not first begin at the start of the twentieth century with the World Missionary Conference in Edinburgh in 1910, which is usually identified as the birth of ecumenism. It begins with humanism, which found the confessional disputes distasteful, and it was anticipated by Melanchthon, Comenius, Leibniz, Bossuet, Pietists, Romantics, the Oxford Movement, and ecumenical prayer and other such movements.[2] With his concern for the universal church, Luther himself does not belong to the period of confessionalism. Therefore, without turning him into an ecumenist in the contemporary sense of the word, one can inquire about his current relevance to ecumenism.

According to the original sense of the word, *ecumene* means the entire inhabited world; therefore, universality in contrast to particularity. One can also say: ecumenism, in contrast to confessionally constricted Catholicism and Protestantism, means the rediscovery of original catholicity without such constriction. For Ignatius of Antioch, who mentions the word *catholic* for the first time in Christian parlance, catholic is where Jesus Christ is.[3] He is the center, the beginning, and the goal of all reality (Eph 1:10; Col 1:15–20). Jesus Christ has reconciled the world with God (2 Cor 5:19). Christian ecumenism is concerned with the unity of the church in service to the unity and peace of the world. It is a matter of universal humanism, which has its foundation in Jesus Christ as the new and final Adam (1 Cor 15:45).

Both churches have ecumenically overcome their denominational self-reference and have learned anew and more deeply how to understand their being Christian in mission, social welfare work, and Christian responsibility for the world as a gift to be handed on. The Catholic Church understands itself as a *sacrament for the world* and it knows that the church, according to its essence, is missionary. Since the General Assembly of the World Council of Churches in Uppsala in 1968, the Protestant churches have completed a similar turn and have broken up the one-sided concentration and narrow focus upon the justification of the individual.[4] The encyclical *Laudato si'* (2015) has broadened once again this universal horizon ecologically and cosmologically.

This ecumenical expansion has led in ecumenism to the discovery that what binds us together in one baptism in Jesus Christ is more than what divides us, and that where we are still divided, we continue to learn from one another. Today both churches understand themselves as *ecclesia semper renovanda et reformanda* [a church always in need of renewal and reform].[5] In this way, Catholics have learned from Protestants the importance of the Word of God and the Bible, and Protestants have learned the importance of sacramental symbolism and liturgy. Both churches have been enriched by ecumenism. In the question of how to understand church and ecclesial office, with which the division of the churches began, divisive differences remain today.

Since the 1970s, these ecclesiological differences have led in the ecumenical movement to two different developments that, at the moment, are mutually inhibiting. On the Protestant side, especially in the "Community of Protestant Churches in Europe" (Leuenberg Agreement of 1973), a model of ecclesial community was developed, based on the mutual recognition of previously separated denominational churches through the acceptance of pulpit and table fellowship.[6] On the Catholic side, bilateral dialogues with the separated churches were begun after the Second Vatican Council. On the German level, the most important dialogue was *Lehrverurteilungen— kirchentrennend?*[7] (1986); on the international level, the *Joint Declaration on the Doctrine of Justification* (1999).[8]

The dialogues have shown that many of the antitheses between the churches rest upon misunderstandings; others no longer apply to the contemporary partner in dialogue; and in yet others, despite remaining differences, convergences can be seen. Because no full consensus was possible, especially concerning the issue of the essence of unity, and concretely the question of office, the results of the dialogues have unfortunately remained fruitless to a great extent in the life of the churches.[9]

The fundamental problem is that the Protestant model of church fellowship and the Catholic model of church unity in Word, Sacrament, and episcopal office (and Petrine ministry), which is dedicated to Word and Sacrament, are not compatible. We are in agreement that we want unity, but we are not in agreement about what constitutes unity. Therefore, we are not in agreement about where the ecumenical journey is supposed to lead. A common ecumenical vision is missing,[10] and sometimes also a common will. Too often we still feel too secure in our own denominational ecclesial fortress. We think that we can still entrench ourselves behind the old ramparts, although they crumbled long ago and the majority of people who once lived in the fortress have long since been living elsewhere.

Thus, the ecumenical momentum of the twentieth century has languished in the meantime. A retreat to confessionalism, however, would be a catastrophe. For in the Western world, a completely different "secular ecumenism" is spreading, for which denominational differences don't matter and which would like to push Christianity out of the public sphere. The much-invoked global world order threatens to become world disorder, in which religious-cultural differences are politically instrumentalized and lead to incredible outbreaks of violence. In many parts of the world, we are experiencing an *ecumene* of blood, which doesn't care about denominational differences: Christians are being persecuted and killed, not because they are Orthodox, Protestant, or Catholic, but simply because they are Christians (Pope Francis). The churches can no longer afford to stand against each other or even to stand self-sufficiently alongside each other; they must live with one another and reach out to one another.

In this situation, ecumenism is challenged anew. Together we must offer the universal Christian message of love and peaceful advocacy for justice, peace, and freedom in opposition to the brutal violence that often uses religion as a smokescreen. The best ecumenical idea for 2017 that I know is, therefore, to celebrate a joint Christ festival (Heinrich Bedford-Strohm). That would be a kind of ecumenical catholicity that is very close to the people and is situated in the midst of the world.

With this, we are confronted with the question: What does Martin Luther have to say to us today about ecumenism?

NOTES

1. Gustav Adolf Benrath and Carl Andresen, eds., *Handbuch der Dogmen- und Theologiegeschichte*, vols. 1–3 (Göttingen: Vandenhoeck & Ruprecht, 1980–1984).

2. J. F. Werling, "Bemühungen um die christliche Einheit in

der Neuzeit," in *Handbuch der Ökumenik*, ed. Hans Jörg Urban and Harald Wagner (Paderborn: Bonifatius, 1985), 307–24.

3. Ignatius of Antioch, To the Smyrnaeans, 8, 2. Concerning an understanding of catholicity, see Walter Kasper, *The Catholic Church: Nature, Reality, and Mission* (New York: Bloomsbury, 2015), 174–82.

4. See the documents of the Second Vatican Council: *Lumen gentium* (Dogmatic Constitution on the Church), 1, 9, 48, and 59; *Gaudium et spes* (Pastoral Constitution on the Church in the Modern World), 42 and 45; *Ad gentes* (Decree on the Church's Missionary Activity), 1f. Compare with Norman Goodall, ed., *Bericht aus Uppsala 1968* (Geneva: World Council of Churches, 1968).

5. See Second Vatican Council, *Lumen gentium*, 8; *Unitatis redintegratio* (Decree on Ecumenism), 4 and 6. Compare with Groupe des Dombes, *Für die Umkehr der Kirchen: Identität und Wandel im Vollzug der Kirchengemeinschaft* (Frankfurt am Main: Lembeck, 1994).

6. A. Birmelé, "Die Ekklesiologie der Leuenberger Kirchengemeinschaft" in *Kirche in ökumenischer Perspektive: Kardinal Walter Kasper zum 70. Geburtstag*, ed. Peter Walter, Klaus Krämer, and George Augustin (Freiburg im Breisgau: Herder, 2003), 46–61.

7. Karl Lehmann and Wolfhart Pannenberg, *Lehrverurteilungen—kirchentrennend?* vol. 1: *Rechtfertigung, Sakramente und Amt im Zeitalter der Reformation und heute* (Freiburg im Breisgau: Herder, 1986). See also volumes 2–4 (1989–1994) as well, with materials and responses to the different positions. Only volume 1 has been translated into English: Karl Lehmann and Wolfhart Pannenberg, eds., *The Condemnations of the Reformation Era: Do They Still Divide?* (Minneapolis: Fortress Press, 1990).

8. *Joint Declaration on the Doctrine of Justification* (1999). The World Methodist Council affirmed the Joint Declaration at its meeting in Seoul, Korea on July 23, 2006. Compare with *10 Jahre Gemeinsame Erklärung zur Rechtfertigungslehre/10 Years Joint Declaration on the Doctrine of Justification* (Paderborn: Bonifatius, 2011). See the article from Karl Lehmann on pages 77–104, which provides an excellent overview of the international preparations and the fundamental theological principles of the Declaration.

9. Walter Kasper, *Harvesting the Fruits: Basic Aspects of Christian Faith in Ecumenical Dialogue* (New York: Continuum,

2009); John A. Radano, ed., *Celebrating a Century of Ecumenism: Exploring the Achievements of International Dialogue* (Grand Rapids: Eerdmans, 2012).

10. The study of the Faith and Order Commission of the World Council of Churches is helpful in this regard and moves forward: *Die Kirche: Auf dem Weg zu einer gemeinsamen Vision* (Paderborn: Bonifatius, 2014).

Chapter 6

MARTIN LUTHER'S ECUMENICAL RELEVANCE

Luther was not an ecumenist in the contemporary sense. Just as little were his opponents. Both tended toward polemics and disputes that led to the narrowing and hardening of positions on both sides. Beginning with the question about the righteousness and mercy of God, revealed in the gospel, the issues came to a head quite early on in the question about the church, especially the question about the pope. Because the pope and the bishops refused reform, Luther had to be satisfied with an emergency arrangement on the basis of his understanding of the common priesthood of believers. However, he was confident that the truth of the gospel would be implemented, and therefore, he basically left open the door to a possible rapprochement in the future.

Likewise, at the beginning of the sixteenth century, many things were still open on the Catholic side. There was no well-balanced Catholic ecclesiology, but only approaches that were more like a hierarchology than ecclesiology. The systematic formation of an ecclesiology first came into being in polemical theology, as the antithesis to Reformation polemics against the papacy. In this way, the papacy became a marker of Catholic identity in a way that was not previously known. The respective denominational thesis and antithesis mutually conditioned and blocked each other.[1]

It was only the more recent ecumenism that again opened the door a crack. Dialogue has taken the place of locking horns.

Dialogue does not mean that one throws overboard that which one previously believed to be true. Only those people can conduct a genuine dialogue who have their own point of view, but are, however, ready to listen to one another and to learn from each other. Such a dialogue is not a purely intellectual affair; it is the exchange of gifts.[2] Dialogue in this way presupposes acknowledgment of the truth of the other as well as one's own weaknesses; stating what you believe is the truth, not in a harmful and polemical way, but in love (Eph 4:15); removing the poison of division from controversies and turning them into a gift through which both sides grow together in the original sense of catholicity, recognizing more deeply God's mercy in Jesus Christ and jointly bearing witness to it in the world.

The last council embarked upon this irreversible path[3]—a path, not a finished solution! The reception of the Second Vatican Council, even fifty years after its conclusion, has not come to its end. Pope Francis has introduced a new phase in its reception.[4] He emphasizes a People of God ecclesiology, the people of God on the move, the sense of faith of the people of God, the synodal structure of the church, and he puts into play an interesting new approach for understanding unity. He describes ecumenical unity no longer in terms of concentric circles around the Roman center point, but rather in terms of a polyhedron, that is, a multisurfaced shape that is not a puzzle constructed from many pieces, but rather is a whole entity. If we think of it as a precious stone, it reflects the light which falls upon it in a wonderfully variegated way. In connection with Oscar Cullmann, Pope Francis takes up the concept of *reconciled diversity*.[5] In his Apostolic Exhortation *Evangelii gaudium* (2013), which outlines his agenda, he proceeds from the gospel and demands a conversion not only of individual Christians, but also of the episcopacy and papal primacy. In this way, without mentioning him by name, the original, fundamental concerns of Luther, the gospel of grace and mercy, and the call to conversion and renewal, stand in the center.

Not only the history of the reception of the last council, but also the history of the reception of Luther has long since not come to an end, not even in the Protestant churches. In Protestantism, there is also a forgetfulness of Luther and alienation from him. Think about his teaching concerning the Last Supper and his Eucharistic piety. It shows that Luther decidedly held to a realistic understanding of the Eucharist against Zwingli and it demonstrates that he cannot be consigned to a religion of interiority.[6] Think, moreover, about the mature Luther's understanding of office, his fundamental openness to the historical episcopacy,[7] as well as his statement that he would carry in his hands and kiss the feet of a pope who allows and acknowledges his gospel.[8] Therefore, it is not possible to appeal only to the polemical statements of the young Luther. Rather, for the sake of ecumenical progress, we must and can also take up anew the question of how to understand church, office, and Eucharist and the relationship between them.[9]

It could take us further along if, in the process, we took seriously the mystical aspects of Luther. They can be found not only in the young Luther, but also in the most agreeable of his major Reformation treatises, *On the Freedom of the Christian*.[10] That could open up opportunities for conversation. For unity and reconciliation occur not only in the head, but first of all in the heart, one's personal piety, everyday life, and human encounter.

Expressed more academically: we need a receptive kind of ecumenism that learns from each other.[11] Only by means of it can the Catholic Church concretely and completely realize its catholicity. On the other hand, Luther's original, basically ecumenical concern can also come to completion only by means of receptive ecumenism. We still don't have a joint solution, but a possible common perspective and a common path forward is opening up. The path to full unity is open, even if it may perhaps be long and steep.

NOTES

1. Yves Congar, "Die Lehre von der Kirche: Vom Abendländischen Schisma bis zu Gegenwart," in *Handbuch der Dogmengeschichte* Bd. III/3, ed. Michael Schmaus (Freiburg im Breisgau: Herder, 1971), chapters 2 and 3; Walter Kasper, *The Catholic Church: Nature, Reality and Mission*, trans. Thomas Hoebel (New York: Bloomsbury, 2015), 61–66.

2. Pope John Paul II, *Ut unum sint* (On Commitment to Ecumenism), 28.

3. See Second Vatican Council, *Unitatis redintegratio*; Pope John Paul II, *Ut unum sint*.

4. Walter Kasper, "Die ökumenische Vision von Papst Franziskus," in *Freude an Gott: Auf dem Weg zu einem lebendigen Glauben* (Festschrift für Kurt Kardinal Koch zum 65. Geburtstag), ed. George Augustin and Markus Schulze (Freiburg im Breisgau: Herder, 2015), 19–34.

5. Oscar Cullmann, *Einheit durch Vielfalt: Grundlegung und Beitrag zur Diskussion über die Möglichkeiten ihrer Verwirklichung*, 2nd ed. (Tübingen: Mohr, 1990).

6. Among other texts, see Martin Luther, "Confession Concerning Christ's Supper," in *Luther's Works*, vol. 37: *Word and Sacrament III*, ed. Robert H. Fischer (Philadelphia: Fortress, 1976), 161–372; WA 26: 261–509. The debate with the Catholic position in the sixteenth century was focused more on the sacrificial character of the Mass, concerning which there was then also a lack of clarity on the Catholic side. Today, the opposition can be regarded as alleviated, if not entirely overcome, by means of the more recent theory of anamnesis.

7. See Harding Meyer, "Bemerkungen zum Artikel 28 der Confessio Augustana und zum Artikel 14 der Apologie der Confessio Augustana über das Bischofsamt" in *Versöhnte Verschiedenheit: Aufsätze zur ökumenischen Theologie*, vol. 2: Der katholisch/lutherische Dialog (Frankfurt am Main: Lembeck, 2000), 284–316.

8. Martin Luther, *A Commentary on St. Paul's Epistle to the Galatians*, trans. Theodore Graebner (Grand Rapids: Zondervan, 1949), 53. Cf. Harding Meyer, "Das Papsttum bei Luther und in den lutherischen Bekenntnisschriften," in *Lehrverurteilungen—kirchentrennend?*

vol. 3: *Materialien zur Lehre von den Sakramenten und vom kirchlichen Amt,* ed. Wolfhart Pannenberg (Freiburg im Breisgau: Herder, 1990), 306–28.

9. See U.S. Conference of Catholic Bishops and the Evangelical Lutheran Church in America, *Declaration on the Way: Church, Ministry and Eucharist* (Minneapolis: Augsburg Fortress, 2015).

10. Martin Luther, "The Freedom of a Christian," in *Three Treatises* (Philadelphia: Fortress, 1970), 284–291; WA 7: 20–38; especially, 25f. On this subject: M. Cassese, "La mistica nuziale in Martin Lutero," in *Lutero e la mistica,* ed. Franco Buzzi, Dieter Kampen, and Paolo Ricca (Turin: Claudiana, 2014), 185–230, where reference is made to Luther's dependence upon Augustine, Bernard of Clairvaux, Bonaventure and others.

11. Paul D. Murray, ed., *Receptive Ecumenism and the Call to Catholic Learning: Exploring a Way for Contemporary Ecumenism* (Oxford: OUP, 2008).

Chapter 7

AN ECUMENISM OF MERCY—THE OUTLOOK

The most important contribution of Martin Luther to the furtherance of ecumenism does not lie in his still open ecclesiological approaches, but in his original starting point with the gospel of grace and the mercy of God and the call to conversion. The message of God's mercy was the answer to his personal question and need as well as to the questions of his age. Today, it is also the answer to the signs of the time and the pressing questions of many people. Only God's mercy can heal the deep wounds that the division in the body of Christ (the church) has caused. It can transform and renew our hearts so that we are ready for conversion and for mercifully turning to one another, pardoning the past injustice done to each other, reconciling us and starting us out in order to find ourselves together, walking patiently step by step on the path to unity in reconciled diversity.[1]

In this sense, I would like to build upon a statement that has been put into Martin Luther's mouth. Like the words about the Antichrist, it stands in an eschatological perspective, but is calmer, more relaxed, and hopeful: "If I knew that the world would end tomorrow, I would still plant a little apple tree today." On November 1, 2009, I was allowed to plant a little linden tree in the newly erected Luther garden in Wittenberg. As a return gift, the Lutherans planted, during the term of my successor, a small olive tree at the Roman Basilica of St. Paul Outside-the-Walls.

Whoever plants a sapling has hope, but also needs patience. The sapling must, for a start, grow deeply and establish deep roots so that it can withstand unfavorable storms. We also have to go *ad fontes* [back to the sources] and *ad radices* [back to the roots]. Spiritual ecumenism requires joint reading of Scripture and common prayer. On the other hand, the sapling must grow tall and stretch heavenwards to the light. We cannot make ecumenical Christianity nor engineer or violently force ecumenism. Unity is a gift of God's Holy Spirit. We ought not think too little of his power, or throw in the towel too soon and give up hope before its time. God's Spirit, which has begun the work of unity, will also lead it to its conclusion, a unity not as we want it to be, but rather as He wants it.

Finally, the sapling must grow broadly so that the birds of heaven can nest in its branches (see Matt 13:32), that is, so that all Christians of goodwill can find a place under it and in its shade. We must allow unity in the form of a great, reconciled diversity, corresponding to the figure of the polyhedron, and be open for all people of goodwill and already today give common witness to God and his mercy.

Today, unity is nearer than it was five hundred years ago. It has already begun. In 2017 we are no longer, as was the case in 1517, on the path toward division, but rather on the path to unity. If we have courage and patience, we will not be disappointed in the end. We will rub our eyes and gratefully be amazed at what God's Spirit has brought about, perhaps quite differently from what we have imagined. In this ecumenical perspective, 2017 could be a new opportunity for Protestant as well as for Catholic Christians. We should use it. It would do both churches good and would do good for many people who are waiting for it. And it would do the world good, which especially today needs our common witness.

NOTE

1. See the homily of Pope Francis at the concluding prayer service on January 25, 2016, during the week of prayer for Christian unity: https://w2.vatican.va/content/francesco/en/homilies/2016/documents/ papa-francesco_20160125_vespri-conversione-san-paolo.html

ABOUT THE AUTHOR

WALTER CARDINAL KASPER, born 1933; Doctor of Theology, Professor of Dogmatics; 1989–1999 Bishop of the Diocese of Rottenburg-Stuttgart; elevated to cardinal, 2001; President of the Pontifical Council for the Promotion of Christian Unity and the Commission for Religious Relations with the Jews as well as member of the Congregation for the Doctrine of the Faith and of the Congregation for the Oriental churches.

Walter Cardinal Kasper is the main author of the first volume of the *Katholischer Erwachsenenkatechismus* and the editor-in-chief of the third edition of the *Lexikon für Theologie und Kirche*. His numerous theological publications include: *The God of Jesus Christ; Jesus the Christ; An Introduction to Christian Faith; Theology and Church; The Catholic Church: Nature, Reality, and Mission; Wege zur Einheit der Christen: Schriften zur Ökumene I; Einheit in Jesus Christus: Schriften zur Ökumene II*. His collected works are being published by Herder Publishing in Freiburg-im-Breisgau, Germany.

At his first Angelus address, Pope Francis praised Kasper's book, *Mercy: The Essence of the Gospel and the Key to Christian Life* (Paulist Press, 2014). An aid to understanding Pope Francis' pontificate was published in 2015: *Pope Francis' Revolution of Tenderness and Love: Theological Roots and Pastoral Perspectives* (Paulist Press, 2015).